TRUTH UNVEILED

A Biblical Guide to Discerning Truth Through the Holy Spirit

CJ LESTER

PREFACE

In a time when celebrity pastors fill stadiums and false prophets gather millions of followers through social media, the ability to discern genuine biblical truth from clever deception is more critical than ever. Truth Unveiled stands as both a warning signal and a guiding light for believers navigating today's spiritual challenges.

Grounded in scripture, with references to powerful passages like Matthew 24:24 and 1 Timothy 4:1-2, this book boldly addresses the increasing prevalence of false teachings while providing a roadmap to authentic biblical understanding. But it doesn't stop at exposing deception. Through a transformation in the Bible, Truth Unveiled equips readers to properly navigate the myriad complications of contemporary faith. By examining the scripture more closely, one can develop their foundation in the truth and learn to spot subtle indications of warped teaching and false prophesy.

At its core, this book is about empowering believers with spiritual discernment. It shows how a Spirit-led study of God's Word can deepen faith and help Christians move beyond reliance on charismatic personalities or popular trends. Instead, readers will learn to build a genuine, Scripture-based relationship with God, guided by the Holy Spirit. This path is crucial for learning to trust divine wisdom over human insight and comprehending why some popular beliefs deviate from biblical truth.

Truth Unveiled is not just a critique of false teachings; it is written with courage and empathy. It gives believers the means to learn and comprehend God's Word for themselves. The emphasis is firmly on the Holy Spirit as our truth guide, guiding readers toward biblical understanding while assisting them in avoiding the traps of misleading instruction. "Truth Unveiled" provides the ideal ratio of caution and insight, consistently pointing to the unadulterated truth of God's Word as revealed by His Spirit, whether you're trying to recover from spiritual delusion, fortify your biblical foundation, or just wish to develop your discernment.

INTRODUCTION

Greetings in Christ, I'm CJ Lester by name, and I serve God from my home in Conyers, Georgia, where I am an active member of Conyers Methodist Church. Church. Through my involvement in both my church and the surrounding community, I've had the privilege of witnessing firsthand how truth and deception intertwine in modern Christianity. This book and ministry were born from a burden God placed on my heart - a calling to help His people discern truth from falsehood while growing deeper in their understanding of His Word.

Throughout my spiritual journey, I have often felt a stirring in my heart regarding the state of modern Christianity. As I spent time in prayer and the study of God's Word, I began to realize that many believers today are longing for pure, uncompromised biblical teaching. I saw it clearly—many Christians are scrolling through social media, tuning in to popular TV preachers, and following influential religious voices. Still, there is a hunger in their hearts for something deeper, more authentic. God revealed to me that this hunger exists because many are being fed half-truths instead of the full, unaltered counsel of His Word. This revelation sparked the birth of this ministry, a mission aimed at equipping God's people with the tools to discern genuine biblical teaching from the cleverly disguised falsehoods that so often surround us.

The Holy Spirit has made it clear that this work isn't just about identifying what's the errors in other teachings or ministries. Rather, it's about leading people to a deeper understanding of God's Word while helping them recognize teachings that may lead them astray. As Jesus warned in ***Matthew 24:24, "For false messiahs and false prophets will appear and perform great signs and wonders to deceive, if possible, even the elect."*** This verse has become a cornerstone of our ministry's purpose. We must remain vigilant, for deception is everywhere.

My approach is straightforward - I rely on the Holy Spirit's guidance to illuminate Scripture and seek to reveal God's truth. This isn't about personal opinions or interpretations; it's about allowing God's Word and His Spirit to speak directly to our hearts. As ***1 Timothy 4:1-2 reminds us, "The Spirit clearly says that in later times some will abandon the faith and follow deceiving spirits and things taught by demons. Such teachings come through hypocritical liars, whose consciences have been seared as with a hot iron."*** These words underscore the gravity of the mission before us. We cannot afford to be passive in our pursuit of truth.

Over the years, through my work at Conyers Methodist Church and various community activities, I've developed a deep appreciation for how truth must be delivered with both conviction and compassion. This ministry aims to strike that balance - being bold enough to speak truth when necessary while maintaining the love and grace that characterize Christ's teaching.

This book and the ministry it represents come from a place of genuine concern for God's people. It's not about building a personal platform or gaining followers. Instead, it's about creating a resource that helps believers understand and apply God's Word while avoiding the pitfalls of deceptive teaching. With the Holy Spirit as our guide, we'll explore what Scripture really says about various topics that often get distorted in modern teaching.

My promise to you, the reader, is this: everything we discuss here will be anchored firmly in Scripture, led by the Holy Spirit, and focused on building up the body of Christ. We will not stray from God's truth, no matter how enticing or persuasive the alternatives may seem. Together, we'll learn to discern truth from error, always keeping our eyes fixed on Jesus, the author and perfecter of our faith.

1

WALKING IN TRUTH, LED BY THE SPIRIT

At the very foundation of this ministry lies one key principle—the importance of being led by the Holy Spirit. When I speak of being Spirit-led, I'm not talking about following emotional impulses or claiming special revelations. Rather, I'm referring to the divine guidance promised in ***John 16:13***, where Jesus said***, "But when he, the Spirit of truth, comes, he will guide you into all the truth. He will not speak on his own; he will speak only what he hears, and he will tell you what is yet to come."***

Being led by the Spirit is not a mystical or abstract concept. It is an invitation to submit to God's guidance through careful study of His Word, prayer, and spiritual discernment. The Holy Spirit never contradicts Scripture; instead, He illuminates biblical truth and helps us apply it correctly. ***In Romans 8:14, we read, "For those who the Spirit of God leads are the children of God."*** This leadership isn't mystical or mysterious - it's practical and grounded in God's Word.

In today's world of instant messages and viral sermons, many claim to be speaking by the Spirit while teaching things that clearly contradict Scripture. This is why *1 John 4:1* instructs us to ***"test the spirits to see whether they are from God because many false prophets have gone out into the world."*** The Holy Spirit helps us in this testing process. He aligns our understanding with God's written Word, which serves as the ultimate standard of truth.

My commitment to this ministry is to rely on the Spirit's guidance in several specific ways:

i. **Bible study** - spending time in God's Word not just to gather information but to seek understanding through the Spirit's illumination. ***As 1 Corinthians 2:14 tells us, "The person without the Spirit does not accept the things that come from the Spirit of God but considers them foolishness."***

ii. **Prayer** - maintaining constant communication with God, seeking His wisdom and direction for every teaching and every word written or spoken. James 1:5 promises, "If any of you lacks wisdom, you should ask God, who gives generously to all without finding fault."

iii. **Community** - recognizing that the Spirit often speaks through the counsel of other faithful believers. ***Proverbs 11:14 reminds us that "in the multitude of counselors, there is safety."***

iv. **Discernment** - developing and exercising spiritual discernment to recognize truth from error. Hebrews 5:14 speaks of those "who by constant use have trained themselves to distinguish good from evil."

The Spirit's guidance isn't about adding to Scripture or receiving new revelations. Instead, it's about rightly understanding and applying the truth God has already given us in His Word. This is vital because many false teachers today claim special revelations that contradict or add to Scripture, violating the warning in Revelation 22:18-19.

When the Spirit truly leads us, the fruit becomes evident. Galatians 5:22-23 describes this fruit as "love, joy, peace, forbearance, kindness, goodness, faithfulness, gentleness and self-control." These qualities should mark both our teaching and our approach to exposing false doctrine.

Through this ministry, I aim to demonstrate what Spirit-led teaching looks like - not through claims of special revelation or dramatic experiences, but through careful, prayerful exposition of God's Word, always testing everything against Scripture itself.

2

WHAT THE CHURCH SHOULD AND SHOULD NOT BE

When we examine many churches today, we often find sanctuaries that have strayed far from their divine purpose. The prophet Ezekiel once had a vision in which God showed him the abominations in the temple, saying, ***"Son of man, do you see what they are doing—the utterly detestable things?" (Ezekiel 8:6).*** Like Ezekiel, we must examine what practices have crept into our modern churches that deviate from God's intended purpose.

Perhaps one of the most troubling trends is the transformation of God's house into something that resembles more of a concert venue or political arena than a place of worship. The prophet Amos spoke of such times when he declared, ***"I hate, I despise your religious festivals; your assemblies are a stench to me" (Amos 5:21)***. God wasn't rejecting worship itself. He was condemning worship that had lost its true essence and purpose.

Many churches today have become entertainment centers, dimming their lights to create concert-like atmospheres. They use fog machines and elaborate stage setups that seem more suited for a rock concert than a house of worship. Yet Jesus proclaimed, ***"I am the light of the world" (John 8:12), and Paul reminds us that "God is light; in him there is no darkness at all" (1 John 1:5).*** The church should reflect this characteristic of God Himself. After all, we are called to be ***"children of light" (Ephesians 5:8) and a "city on a hill that cannot be hidden" (Matthew 5:14)***, standing as a beacon of truth and holiness in a world of darkness.

The commercialization of church spaces mirrors the situation Jesus confronted in the temple. He declared, ***"My house will be called a house of prayer, but you are making it a den of robbers" (Matthew 21:13)***. This wasn't just about money changing; it was about the fundamental purpose of God's house being corrupted. Similarly, Peter warned about false teachers who would ***"exploit you with fabricated stories"*** for financial gain ***(2 Peter 2:3).***

The political infiltration of church spaces represents another serious deviation. When the Pharisees attempted to entangle Jesus in politics, asking about taxes to Caesar, His response clearly separated spiritual truth from political maneuvering (Matthew 22:21). The Apostle Paul emphasized that our true citizenship is in heaven (Philippians 3:20), yet too many churches today seem more concerned with earthly politics than with the eternal truths of Scripture.

So, what should the church be? The early church model in *Acts 2:42-47* provides a comprehensive picture: ***"They devoted themselves to the apostles' teaching and fellowship, to the breaking of bread and prayer. Everyone was filled with awe at the many wonders and signs performed by the apostles. All the believers were together and had everything in common... Every day, they continued to meet together in the temple courts. They broke bread in their homes and ate together with glad and sincere hearts, praising God and enjoying the favor of all the people."***

The church should be a house of prayer where, as Isaiah prophesied, ***"my house shall be called a house of prayer for all peoples" (Isaiah 56:7)***. It must be a sanctuary for true worship where, as Jesus said, ***"true worshipers will worship the Father in the Spirit and truth" (John 4:23)***. The focus should be on honoring God, not creating a spectacle.

Regarding finances, Paul provided clear direction: ***"On the first day of every week, each one of you should set aside a sum of money in keeping with your income" (1 Corinthians 16:2)***. This was for the work of ministry, not for creating spectacles. As Paul reminded Timothy, ***"Godliness with contentment is great gain" (1 Timothy 6:6)***.

The early church met in homes and simple buildings. Yet, they were described as those who ***"turned the world upside down" (Acts 17:6)***. Their power came not from elaborate productions but from the presence of God, fulfilling Christ's promise: "For where two or three gather in my name, there am I with them" (Matthew 18:20). When we gather in humility and reverence, we invite the fullness of His presence into our midst.

Let us remember Solomon's wisdom when he dedicated the first temple: ***"But will God really dwell on earth with humans? The heavens, even the highest heavens, cannot contain you. How much less this temple I have built!" (2 Chronicles 6:18).*** This humility should characterize our approach to church, recognizing that no amount of production value can substitute for God's presence.

The church is not meant to be a theater, political headquarters, or marketplace. Still, as Paul wrote to Timothy, it should be ***"the pillar and foundation of the truth" (1 Timothy 3:15)***. When we return to these fundamental principles, we create space for genuine encounters with God, unhindered by worldly distractions or commercial interests.

3

MODERN FALSE TEACHINGS AND HOW TO IDENTIFY THEM

Scripture warns us repeatedly about the danger of false teachings entering the church. As Paul wrote to Timothy, *"For time will come when people will not put up with sound doctrine. Instead, to suit their desires, they will gather around them a great number of teachers to say what their itching ears want to hear" (2 Timothy 4:3).* This prophecy has never been more relevant than in our current age.

Biblical Tests for Identifying False Teaching

First and foremost, any teaching must align with the character and nature of God as revealed in Scripture. John provides us with a fundamental test in *1 John 4:1-3: "Dear friends, do not believe every spirit, but test the spirits to see whether they are from God because many false prophets have gone out into the world. This is how you can recognize the Spirit of God: Every spirit that acknowledges that Jesus Christ has come in the flesh is from God, but every spirit that does not acknowledge Jesus is not from God."*

Here are the biblical standards for testing and teaching:

i. **The Jesus Test:** Does the teaching align with the biblical Jesus? Paul warns in 2 Corinthians 11:4, "For if someone comes to you and preaches a Jesus other than the Jesus we preached, or if you receive a different spirit from the Spirit you received, or a different gospel from the one you accepted, you put up with it easily enough."

ii. **The Gospel Test:** Is the gospel of salvation by grace through faith being preserved? As Paul firmly stated in *Galatians 1:8-9: "But even if we or an angel from heaven should preach a gospel other than the one we preached to you, let them be under God's curse!* As we have already said, so now I say again: If anybody is preaching to you a gospel other than what you accepted, let them be under God's curse!"

iii. **The Scripture Test:** Does the teaching align with the whole of Scripture? *"All Scripture is God-breathed and is useful for teaching, rebuking, correcting and training in righteousness" (2 Timothy 3:16).* Any teaching that contradicts or adds to Scripture must be rejected.

iv. **The Fruit Test:** Jesus taught in *Matthew 7:15-20, "Watch out for false prophets. They come to you in sheep's clothing, but inwardly, they are ferocious wolves. By their fruit, you will recognize them... Every good tree bears good fruit, but a bad tree bears bad fruit."*

v. **The Lifestyle Test:** Do the teachers' lives reflect godly character? "But the wisdom that comes from heaven is first of all pure; then peace-loving, considerate, submissive, full of mercy and good fruit, impartial and sincere" (James 3:17).

vi. **The Love Test:** Does the teaching promote genuine love for God and others? *"If I speak in the tongues of men or of angels, but do not have love, I am only a resounding gong or a clanging cymbal" (1 Corinthians 13:1).*

Remember Paul's warning to the Colossians: *"See to it that no one takes you captive through hollow and deceptive philosophy, which depends on human tradition and the elemental spiritual forces of this world rather than on Christ" (Colossians 2:8).*

When examining any teaching, we must follow the example of the Bereans, who *"received the message with great eagerness and examined the Scriptures every day to see if what Paul said was true" (Acts 17:11)*. This diligent examination of Scripture remains our surest defense against false teaching.

In our current age, many teach what the apostle Peter warned about: "There will be false teachers among you. They will secretly introduce destructive heresies... Many will follow their depraved conduct and will bring the way of truth into disrepute. In their greed, these teachers will exploit you with fabricated stories" (2 Peter 2:1-3).

The antidote to false teaching remains the same as it was in the early church: a thorough knowledge of Scripture, reliance on the Holy Spirit's guidance, and a commitment to testing everything against God's Word. As John wrote, ***"Dear friends, do not believe every spirit, but test the spirits to see whether they are from God" (1 John 4:1).***

I've also created an easy way for people to use when they are trying to find a church home or just trying to follow another ministry. Here it is:

The SPIRIT Test: Your Guide to Discerning Truth

The SPIRIT Test is a simple, Scripture-based method to help you evaluate any teaching, church, or ministry:

S - Scripture Alignment: "Does this teaching align with the whole of Scripture?" Key Verse: ***"All Scripture is God-breathed and is useful for teaching, rebuking, correcting and training in righteousness" (2 Timothy 3:16)***

P - Prophetic Accuracy: "Are their prophecies 100% accurate and Christ-centered?" Key Verse: ***"Watch out for false prophets. They come to you in sheep's clothing, but inwardly they are ferocious wolves" (Matthew 7:15)***

I - Integrity in Leadership: "Do the leaders demonstrate godly character and transparency?" Key Verse*:* ***"An elder must be blameless, faithful to his wife, a man whose children believe and are not open to the charge of being wild and disobedient" (Titus 1:6)***

R - Reliable Gospel Message: "Is salvation by grace through faith being taught?" Key Verse: *"For it is by grace you have been saved, through faith—and this is not from yourselves, it is the gift of God" (Ephesians 2:8)*

I - Income/Money Focus: "Is there excessive focus on money or prosperity?" Key Verse: *"For the love of money is a root of all kinds of evil" (1 Timothy 6:10)*

T - True to Jesus's Nature: "Is Jesus Christ presented as revealed in Scripture?" Key Verse: *"Every spirit that acknowledges that Jesus Christ has come in the flesh is from God" (1 John 4:2)*

Quick Assessment Questions:

1. Do they add to or subtract from Scripture?
2. Is money frequently emphasized?
3. Do they claim exclusive new revelations?
4. Is their focus on Christ or personalities?
5. Do they pressure people for donations?
6. Are they accountable and transparent?

Remember: Print this guide and keep it in your Bible. When visiting a new church or following a ministry online, take time to apply each element of the SPIRIT Test. Don't rush your evaluation - pray and allow the Holy Spirit to guide you through this process.

Warning Signs That Should Raise Immediate Concern:

1. Pressure to give money for "special blessings"
2. Claims of exclusive revelations not found in Scripture
3. Prophecies that don't come true or contradict Scripture
4. Leadership that resists questions or accountability
5. Teaching that contradicts the clear biblical doctrine

Jesus warned us: "For false messiahs and false prophets will appear and perform great signs and wonders to deceive, if possible, even the elect" (Matthew 24:24). Use this SPIRIT Test as your practical tool for discernment in these challenging times.

The Once Saved Always Saved Doctrine: A Closer Examination

One prevalent teaching, particularly within Independent Fundamental Baptist and some Southern Baptist churches, is the doctrine of "once saved, always saved" or eternal security. While rooted in a desire to emphasize God's faithfulness, this teaching often gets distorted into a dangerous misunderstanding of salvation and discipleship.

Proponents often cite verses like John 10:28-29: "I give them eternal life, and they shall never perish; no one will snatch them out of my hand. My Father, who has given them to me, is greater than all; no one can snatch them out of my Father's hand." While these verses beautifully express God's protection, they're sometimes used to justify a belief that any profession of faith, regardless of subsequent lifestyle, guarantees eternal salvation.

Let's examine this through Scripture:

Jesus taught in ***Matthew 7:21-23: "Not everyone who says to me, 'Lord, Lord,' will enter the kingdom of heaven, but only the one who does the will of my Father who is in heaven. Many will say to me on that day, 'Lord, Lord, did we not prophesy in your name and your name drive out demons and in your name perform many miracles?' Then I will tell them plainly, 'I never knew you. Away from me, you evildoers!'"***

The Apostle Paul expressed concern about his salvation in ***1 Corinthians 9:27: "I strike a blow to my body and make it my slave so that after I have preached to others, I will not be disqualified for the prize."***

James emphasizes that faith without works is dead ***(James 2:17): "In the same way, faith by itself, if it is not accompanied by action, is dead."*** He further explains that even demons believe in God (James 2:19), showing that mere intellectual assent isn't sufficient for salvation.

The danger of this teaching lies in its potential misuse:

1. It can lead to casual Christianity where personal holiness is seen as optional
2. It might create false security based on a one-time prayer or altar call
3. It can minimize the biblical calls to perseverance and faithful living
4. It potentially separates salvation from discipleship, which Jesus never did

SPIRIT Test Application:

1. Scripture Alignment: Selectively uses verses while ignoring others about perseverance
2. Prophetic Accuracy: Often dismisses biblical warnings about falling away
3. Integrity: Can lead to compromised living
4. Reliable Gospel: May reduce the gospel to a one-time decision
5. Income Focus: Less emphasis here
6. True to Jesus: Often ignores His teachings about counting the cost and bearing fruit

The biblical truth balances God's faithfulness with our responsibility. *Philippians 2:12-13 captures this tension: "Continue to work out your salvation with fear and trembling, for it is God who works in you to will and to act in order to fulfill his good purpose."*

True salvation produces transformation. As Paul states in ***2 Corinthians 5:17: "Therefore, if anyone is in Christ, the new creation has come: The old has gone, the new is here!"*** While we can have assurance of salvation, this assurance comes through ongoing evidence of God's work in our lives, not merely a past decision.

This teaching reminds us why we must carefully examine all doctrines, even those from respected denominational traditions, against the full counsel of Scripture. As Peter warned, ***"There will be false teachers among you" (2 Peter 2:1)***, and these can come from any theological background.

Examining United Pentecostal Church (UPC) Doctrine Through the SPIRIT Test

One significant teaching that needs careful examination comes from the United Pentecostal Church (UPC), which teaches that salvation requires:

1. Baptism specifically in Jesus' name only (rejecting trinitarian baptism)
2. Speaking in tongues as evidence of receiving the Holy Spirit
3. Both are required for salvation

Let's apply our SPIRIT Test:

i. **Scripture Alignment:** The UPC teaching contradicts clear biblical examples of salvation. The thief on the cross (Luke 23:39-43) was promised paradise by Jesus without baptism or tongues. In Acts 10:44-48, Cornelius and his household received the Holy Spirit and spoke in tongues before being baptized, showing these aren't prerequisites for salvation.

ii. **Prophetic Accuracy:** While UPC doesn't focus on prophecy, its interpretation of Acts 2:38 ("Repent and be baptized every one of you in the name of Jesus Christ") as an exclusive baptismal formula contradicts Matthew 28:19, where Jesus commands baptism "in the name of the Father and of the Son and the Holy Spirit."

iii. **Integrity in Leadership:** While many UPC leaders are sincere, their teaching adds requirements to salvation beyond what Scripture requires.

iv. **Reliable Gospel:** This teaching severely distorts the gospel by adding works-based requirements. Paul clearly states in Ephesians 2:8-9: "For by grace you have been saved through faith, and that not of yourselves; it is the gift of God, not of works, lest anyone should boast."

v. **Income/Money Focus:** This isn't typically an issue in UPC teachings.

vi. **True to Jesus's Nature:** The UPC's rejection of the Trinity and insistence on "Jesus only" baptism contradicts the full biblical revelation of God's nature. Jesus Himself was baptized with the Father speaking and the Spirit descending (Matthew 3:16-17).

Key Scriptures That Refute This Teaching:

1. *Romans 10:9-10: "If you confess with your mouth that Jesus is Lord and believe in your heart that God raised him from the dead, you will be saved."*
2. *Ephesians 1:13: "When you believed, you were marked in him with a seal, the promised Holy Spirit."*
3. *Acts 16:31: "Believe in the Lord Jesus, and you will be saved."*

This teaching exemplifies why the SPIRIT Test is crucial. While appearing spiritual and biblical on the surface, it adds requirements to salvation that Scripture itself doesn't demand, potentially leading people away from the simple gospel truth of salvation by grace through faith in Jesus Christ alone.

Remember Jesus's warning about adding to God's requirements: *"They worship me in vain; their teachings are merely human rules" (Matthew 15:9).*

A Personal Note on Speaking in Tongues

While examining these teachings, I want to make my position clear. I do believe in speaking in tongues and recognize it as initial evidence of the Holy Spirit's baptism, as we see demonstrated throughout the book of Acts. The experience is real and biblical, occurring multiple times in Scripture (Acts 2, Acts 10, Acts 19).

However, we must maintain biblical balance. I firmly believe that speaking in tongues, while a genuine gift from God, is not a requirement for salvation or entrance into heaven. The Bible is clear that salvation comes through faith in Jesus Christ: ***"For it is by grace you have been saved through faith, and this is not from yourselves, it is the gift of God" (Ephesians 2:8).***

The Apostle Paul himself addresses this in ***1 Corinthians 12:29-30 when he asks rhetorically, "Are all apostles? Are all prophets? Are all teachers? Do all work miracles? Do all have gifts of healing? Do all speak in tongues? Do all interpret?"*** The implied answer is clearly no. If speaking in tongues were required for salvation, Paul's statement wouldn't make sense.

We must be careful not to elevate any spiritual gift, including tongues, to a position that Scripture doesn't give it. The gospel's simplicity is its beauty - salvation through faith in Christ alone. Adding requirements beyond this, no matter how spiritual they may seem, risks distorting the pure message of God's grace.

In 1 Corinthians 13:1, Paul reminds us that even speaking in tongues without love is meaningless. Our focus should be on leading people to a genuine relationship with Jesus Christ, allowing the Holy Spirit to work in their lives as He sees fit.

4

THE TRUTH ABOUT MINISTRY AND MONEY: A BIBLICAL PERSPECTIVE

Money in ministry remains one of the most misunderstood and often exploited topics in modern Christianity. While some false teachers turn the gospel into a means of financial gain, others avoid discussing ministry finances altogether. Let us examine this topic through the clear lens of Scripture, separating truth from exploitation.

Scripture provides a balanced view of ministry finances. The Apostle Paul writes in ***1 Timothy 5:18, "For Scripture says, 'Do not muzzle an ox while it is treading out the grain,' and 'The worker deserves his wages.'" This principle acknowledges that legitimate ministry work deserves appropriate support. Yet the same Paul also proclaimed in 2 Corinthians 2:17, "Unlike so many, we do not peddle the word of God for profit." Ministry should never be about making money.***

The truth is simple: ministry requires resources. There are practical costs involved in spreading the gospel in today's digital age. Our ministry faces real expenses in fulfilling its mission. We invest in creating digital flyers to spread awareness, maintaining a website that hosts our blogs and messages for followers, and publishing books that share biblical truth. These resources help us reach people effectively with God's message. Each step in the publishing process itself - from writing to editing to distribution - requires financial investment to ensure God's truth reaches those who need it most.

Jesus Himself had supporters who "helped to support them out of their means" (Luke 8:3). The early church also shared resources to ensure the gospel could spread effectively (Acts 4:32-35). Today, we follow their example, using resources wisely to maximize our reach—both through traditional and modern methods.

This biblical understanding stands in contrast to the exploitation we often see today. When ministries demand "seed faith" gifts with promises of multiplied returns, they distort the gospel's message. When leaders live in luxury while their congregations struggle, they forsake the servant heart of Jesus, who *"though he was rich, yet for your sake he became poor" (2 Corinthians 8:9).*

In our ministry, we are committed to financial transparency. Every dollar we receive is used to spread God's Word through our platforms and publications. As Paul wrote, we *"aim at what is honorable not only in the Lord's sight but also in the sight of man" (2 Corinthians 8:21).*

We reject the prosperity gospel and manipulative fundraising tactics. We will never promise financial blessings in exchange for donations or use pressure to solicit funds. The gospel is not for sale, and God's blessings cannot be purchased.

We are careful stewards of the resources God provides. This means making thoughtful decisions about expenses, investing in necessary tools for ministry outreach, and ensuring funds primarily support spreading God's Word rather than administrative overhead. Each investment, whether in digital resources, website maintenance, or book publication, serves to further our mission of sharing biblical truth.

Jesus spoke more about money than about almost any other topic—not because money itself is evil, but because our attitude toward it reveals our hearts. A biblical ministry must balance acknowledging legitimate financial needs while avoiding the love of money that has destroyed so many ministries.

Ministry is never about money. It's about faithfully serving God and spreading His truth. Yet, just as a farmer needs tools to work in his field, the ministry requires resources to function effectively in today's world. The key lies in maintaining biblical balance - neither ignoring practical needs nor allowing them to overshadow the gospel's central message of salvation through Christ alone.

Applying The SPIRIT Test to Ministry Finances

Careful discernment is essential when evaluating any ministry's financial practices or teachings about money. Jesus spoke extensively about money, not because it was central to His message but because He understood how it could corrupt the hearts of both leaders and followers. Let's apply our SPIRIT Test to examine financial teachings and practices in ministry.

The SPIRIT Test for Ministry Finances:

- S - Scripture Alignment Does their teaching about money align with the whole of Scripture? Key Verse: *"For the love of money is a root of all kinds of evil. Some people, eager for money, have wandered from the faith and pierced themselves with many griefs"* (1 Timothy 6:10)
- P - Prophetic Accuracy: Are financial "prophecies" and promises biblical or manipulative? Key Verse: "But there were also false prophets among the people, just as there will be false teachers among you... In their greed these teachers will exploit you with fabricated stories" (2 Peter 2:1-3)
- I - Integrity in Leadership: Is there financial transparency and accountability? Key Verse: *"For we are taking pains to do what is right, not only in the eyes of the Lord but also in the eyes of man"* (2 Corinthians 8:21)
- R - Reliable Gospel: Is the gospel kept pure from financial corruption? Key Verse: *"For by grace you have been saved*

through faith, and this is not from yourselves; it is the gift of God" (Ephesians 2:8)

- I - Income Focus: Is there an excessive emphasis on money and giving? Key Verse: ***"Each of you should give what you have decided in your heart to give, not reluctantly or under compulsion, for God loves a cheerful giver" (2 Corinthians 9:7)***
- T - True to Jesus's Nature: Does their approach to money reflect Jesus's teaching and example? Key Verse: "No one can serve two masters... ***You cannot serve both God and money" (Matthew 6:24)***

Remember that legitimate ministries need resources to operate, but they will maintain biblical balance, transparency, and integrity in their financial practices. As Jesus reminded us in ***Matthew 10:8, "Freely you have received; freely give."*** Any ministry that places undue emphasis on money or uses manipulation to secure donations fails the SPIRIT Test and requires careful examination.

5

THE HOLY SPIRIT VS. EMOTIONAL MANIPULATION

In today's Christian world, one of the most deceptive challenges is replacing the true work of the Holy Spirit with emotional manipulation. Jesus warned us that not everything spiritual is from God's Spirit, which is why we must ***"test the spirits to see whether they are from God" (1 John 4:1).***

Understanding the true work of the Holy Spirit is essential. To distinguish between the genuine work of the Holy Spirit and emotional manipulation, it's essential to understand what the Spirit's work looks like. Jesus provides a clear description in ***John 16:13-14: "But when he, the Spirit of truth, comes, he will guide you into all the truth... He will glorify me because it is from me that he will receive what he will make known to you.***

The genuine work of the Holy Spirit always points to Jesus Christ, aligns with Scripture, produces spiritual fruit as described in Galatians 5:22-23, builds up the church in love, and brings conviction of sin, righteousness, and judgment as Jesus promised in John 16:8. In contrast, emotional manipulation in church settings often manifests through extended music designed to create emotional highs, peer pressure to display certain behaviors, and the use of guilt or fear to prompt responses. Many churches create artificial atmospheres through carefully crafted lighting and effects, employ prolonged repetition to induce altered states, and pressure congregants to "manifest" certain gifts.

The Spirit's genuine work differs fundamentally from emotional manipulation. While the Holy Spirit always glorifies Christ (John 16:14), emotional manipulation often glorifies experiences, feelings, or human personalities. The Spirit produces lasting fruit - love, joy, peace, patience, kindness, goodness, faithfulness, gentleness, and self-control (Galatians 5:22-23), whereas manipulation produces temporary emotional highs followed by confusion or dependency. Furthermore, as Scripture tells us, **"Where the Spirit of the Lord is, there is freedom" (2 Corinthians 3:17).** The Holy Spirit never coerces or manipulates; He invites, guides, and allows free response, while manipulation pressures, shames, or forces responses.

Apostle Paul warns us in 2 Corinthians 11:4 about accepting "a different spirit from the Spirit you received." Many sincere believers, hungry for genuine spiritual experience, can be led astray by counterfeit spiritual manifestations. In the modern church, we often see this through extended altar calls that use emotional music and repetitive phrases to induce responses or through services designed to create an atmosphere of emotional intensity rather than genuine spiritual engagement.

True spiritual experiences will always align with Scripture and point people to Jesus Christ, not to emotional highs or charismatic personalities. The Holy Spirit works to convict of sin and bring genuine repentance, not just emotional responses. His presence brings clarity and peace, not confusion and pressure. Most importantly, genuine spiritual experiences result in lasting transformation and deeper devotion to Christ, not just temporary emotional elevation.

Remember, the Holy Spirit's primary role is to reveal Christ and transform believers into His image, as Paul teaches in 2 Corinthians 3:18. Any spiritual experience that doesn't serve this purpose should be carefully examined. When we understand and apply these biblical principles, we can better discern between genuine moves of the Spirit and emotional manipulation, ensuring our worship remains pure and our experiences authentic.

Let's examine specific examples of genuine Holy Spirit experiences versus emotional manipulation in today's church settings. The Apostle Paul teaches us in *1 Corinthians 14:33* that ***"God is not a God of disorder but of peace."*** This principle helps us identify genuine spiritual experiences.

In genuine Holy Spirit conviction, a person might quietly begin weeping during worship or preaching, not because of emotional music or manipulation, but because God's Spirit is dealing with their heart about specific sins. This conviction leads to genuine repentance and life change, not just an emotional moment at an altar. As Jesus promised in ***John 16:8, "When he comes, he will prove the world to be wrong about sin and righteousness and judgment."***

Consider a worship service where the Holy Spirit is truly present. Rather than being marked by chaos or emotional frenzy, there's often a weighty sense of God's presence that brings deep peace. People may weep quietly or pray deeply, not because of emotional music or repetition, but because the Spirit is working in their hearts, convicting them of sin or drawing them closer to Christ. As the Psalmist wrote, ***"Be still, and know that I am God" (Psalm 46:10).***

Genuine prophecy in church settings doesn't involve theatrical displays or vague, fortune-cookie-style predictions. Instead, it brings specific encouragement, conviction, or direction that aligns perfectly with Scripture. Paul describes this in ***1 Corinthians 14:3: "But the one who prophesies speaks to people for their strengthening, encouraging and comfort."*** The person receiving such a word often experiences deep inner confirmation rather than emotional excitement.

True Holy Spirit baptism, while potentially including speaking in tongues, is fundamentally about empowerment for service and witness, as Jesus promised in Acts 1:8. It's not about creating an emotional experience or proving spiritual status. The evidence appears in transformed lives and bold witness for Christ, not just in momentary manifestations.

In prayer ministry, genuine Holy Spirit work often brings deep peace rather than emotional displays. A person might experience profound inner healing without any outward manifestation. Over time, the fruit becomes evident in their changed relationships and emotional wholeness, fulfilling God's promise in ***Isaiah 61:1*** to ***"bind up the brokenhearted."***

When the Spirit genuinely moves in corporate worship, there's often a supernatural unity that transcends emotional excitement. People might experience a deep awareness of God's love, resulting in spontaneous acts of reconciliation or confession. This fulfills Jesus's prayer in John 17 for supernatural unity among believers.

Remember, the Holy Spirit's work always results in more love for Jesus, greater alignment with Scripture, and lasting life transformation. While emotions may be involved, they are never the focus or the validation of the experience. As Peter demonstrated at Pentecost, genuine spiritual experiences can be explained biblically and point people to Christ, not to the experience itself.

In contrast, manipulated experiences often leave people dependent on the next emotional high, constantly seeking more intense experiences. Genuine Holy Spirit encounters leave people more grounded in Scripture, more stable in their faith, and more effective in their witness for Christ.

6

SOCIAL MEDIA MINISTRY: TRUTH VS. TRENDING

In an era where influence is measured in likes and followers, the church faces unique challenges in maintaining biblical integrity while using modern platforms. Jesus's words in **Matthew 24:24** have new relevance: ***"For false messiahs and false prophets will appear and perform great signs and wonders to deceive, if possible, even the elect."***

Social media has become the modern marketplace where content competes for attention. Platforms like Facebook, Instagram, and TikTok offer unprecedented opportunities to spread the gospel, but they also create unique dangers for biblical truth. Paul's warning in *2 Timothy 4:3-4 seems particularly prophetic: "For the time will come when people will not put up with sound doctrine. Instead, to suit their desires, they will gather around them a great number of teachers to say what their itching ears want to hear. They will turn their ears away from the truth and turn aside to myths."*

Today's "itching ears" of many are drawn to quick, entertaining content instead of sound biblical teaching. Too often, social media ministers prioritize popularity over truth, creating content that entertains rather than enlightens. We see "prophets" posting daily words that tickle ears but lack biblical substance, teachers sharing prosperity messages that go viral while ignoring the full counsel of Scripture, and ministries more concerned with algorithms than accuracy.

This is why I've been called to establish The Truth Broadcast on Facebook and YouTube. This ministry isn't about chasing trends or watering down God's Word to gain followers. Instead, it's a platform where believers can find biblical truth delivered with the power of the Holy Spirit. Each week, I share messages with my followers and faithful supporters that dig deep into God's Word, exposing false teachings while guiding people to genuine biblical truth.

The Truth Broadcast stands apart from typical social media ministries because we refuse to compromise. Our weekly messages tackle difficult topics head-on, led by the Holy Spirit and grounded in Scripture. Whether addressing popular false teachings, examining current trends in Christianity, or providing deep biblical teaching, every broadcast aims to equip believers with the truth.

Through this platform, we're creating a space where:

- God's Word is taught without compromise
- The Holy Spirit's guidance is emphasized
- False teachings are exposed with love and biblical accuracy

- Believers can find answers to challenging questions
- Deep biblical truth replaces surface-level Christianity

My focus isn't on gaining likes or subscribers but on building a community of believers who hunger for truth. When Paul spoke to the Thessalonians, he reminded them, ***"Our appeal does not spring from error or impurity or any attempt to deceive, but just as we have been approved by God to be entrusted with the gospel, so we speak, not to please man, but to please God who tests our hearts" (1 Thessalonians 2:3-4).*** This verse guides every broadcast we produce.

The Truth Broadcast is like a lighthouse in a storm, guiding believers through the fog of false teachings that saturate social media. We examine current trends in Christianity, popular teachings, and viral messages, always testing them against Scripture and providing biblical correction where needed.

In a world where many chase digital popularity, The Truth Broadcast remains committed to its mission to deliver Spirit-filled, biblically sound teaching that transforms lives. Our success isn't measured by social media metrics but by our faithfulness to God's Word and the spiritual growth of our community.

I invite you to join us in spreading biblical truth in the digital age. Together, we can create a space where God's Word is honored, the Holy Spirit is welcome, and truth prevails over trends.

Beyond our Facebook and YouTube presence, The Truth Broadcast ministry extends to our dedicated website, creating a comprehensive digital platform for spreading biblical truth. This website serves as a central hub where believers can find in-depth biblical teaching through our blog posts, access archived messages, and connect more deeply with our ministry's mission.

Our blog provides detailed examinations of biblical topics that require more extensive exploration than social media allows. We delve into Scripture verse by verse, addressing complex theological questions and current issues facing the church. These articles serve as valuable resources for believers seeking to deepen their understanding of God's Word.

The website also offers various ways to interact with our ministry. Visitors can submit prayer requests, ask biblical questions, and engage in meaningful discussions about our teachings. We believe in fostering a community of believers who support one another in their pursuit of truth.

While our primary focus remains delivering God's truth, we understand the practical aspects of running a digital ministry. As discussed in our chapter on ministry finances, the cost of operating a website, producing videos, and purchasing technical equipment is real. For those led by the Spirit to support this work, we provide transparent giving options through our website. However, all our content remains freely available because the truth should never come with a price tag. As Jesus said, ***"Freely you have received; freely give" (Matthew 10:8).***

The Truth Broadcast's online presence - through social media, video content, and our website - represents a unified effort to combat false teaching and promote biblical truth in the digital age. Each platform serves its unique purpose in our larger mission: Facebook and YouTube for immediate engagement and monthly messages and our website for deeper study and community connection.

7

BIBLICAL LEADERSHIP VS CELEBRITY PASTORS

In today's church landscape, we've witnessed the rise of what many call "celebrity pastors," who have become a prominent trend—religious leaders who have gained fame through large platforms, bestselling books, and massive social media followings. While having influence isn't inherently wrong, it is vital that we examine this phenomenon against Scripture's teachings on biblical leadership.

Jesus offered a clear picture of true spiritual leadership in *Matthew 20:25-28: "You know that the rulers of the Gentiles lord it over them, and their great ones exercise authority over them. It shall not be so among you. But whoever would be great among you must be your servant, and whoever would be first among you must be your slave, even as the Son of Man came not to be served but to serve and to give his life as a ransom for many."*

This passage highlights the stark contrast between biblical leadership and the celebrity culture that has infiltrated the church. Biblical leaders follow Jesus's model of servanthood, while celebrity pastors often create empires centered on their personalities. We see pastors arriving at church in luxury cars, wearing designer clothes, and living in mansions while claiming it's all for God's glory. This directly contradicts the example set by the apostles and early church leaders.

Paul described true spiritual leadership in *1 Thessalonians 2:6-7: "We were not looking for praise from people, not from you or anyone else... Instead, we were like young children among you. Just as a nursing mother cares for her children."* This tender, nurturing image sharply contrasts with the corporate, CEO-style leadership prevalent in many megachurches today.

The danger of celebrity pastor culture extends beyond the obvious issues of pride and materialism. When churches become built around personalities rather than Christ, several serious problems emerge:

First, it creates an unhealthy dependency on human leaders. People begin following the pastor's interpretation of Scripture rather than studying God's Word for themselves. Paul warned about this in *1 Corinthians 3:4-5: "For when one says, 'I follow Paul,' and another, 'I follow Apollos,' are you not mere human beings? What, after all, is Apollos? And what is Paul? Only servants, through whom you came to believe."*

Second, it often leads to a lack of accountability. When pastors become celebrities, they often surround themselves with yes-men rather than true accountability partners. Scripture teaches in Proverbs 27:17 that "iron sharpens iron," suggesting the need for genuine peer relationships rather than a circle of admirers.

Third, the pressure to maintain image and popularity can lead to compromised teaching. Rather than preaching the full counsel of God's Word, celebrity pastors might avoid difficult topics that could alienate followers or affect book sales. ***Yet Paul declared in Acts 20:27, "For I have not hesitated to proclaim to you the whole will of God."***

Biblical leadership focuses on:

- Serving rather than being served
- Building up others rather than personal platforms
- Teaching sound doctrine rather than popular messages
- Living modestly rather than extravagantly
- Remaining accountable rather than untouchable
- Pointing people to Christ rather than themselves

As we examine modern church leadership, we must return to these biblical principles. A true shepherd, as described ***in 1 Peter 5:2-4, leads "not pursuing dishonest gain, but eager to serve; not lording it over those entrusted to you, but being examples to the flock."***

The effects of celebrity pastor culture on today's church are profound and concerning. Let's examine some specific problems:

i. **The Multi-Site Model Proble:** Many megachurches now operate multiple locations where thousands gather to watch their celebrity pastor on a video screen. While technology can be useful for spreading the gospel, this model often creates a franchise-style Christianity where personal pastoral care is sacrificed for the sake of brand expansion. Jesus taught His disciples to be shepherds who know their sheep personally (John 10:14), not distant figures on a screen.

ii. **The Merchandising of Ministry:** Walk into many megachurches today, and you'll find bookstores filled with the pastor's latest books, DVD series, study guides, and even clothing lines. While technology can aid in spreading the gospel, this model often sacrifices personal pastoral care for brand expansion. This directly contradicts Peter's warning about shepherds not being greedy for money (1 Peter 5:2).

iii. **Social Media Influence Over Pastoral Care:** Many celebrity pastors spend more time building their social media presence than visiting the sick or counseling their congregation. Some have millions of followers online but wouldn't recognize their church members at the grocery store. Real pastoral ministry, as modeled in Scripture, involves personal involvement in people's lives, not just broadcasting to masses of anonymous followers.

iv. **The "Green Room" Mentality:** In many large churches, pastors have become so isolated they spend their time before and after services in exclusive "green rooms," separated from the congregation. Some even have private entrances and exits to avoid interaction with church members. Compare this to the Apostle Paul, who reminded the Ephesian elders that he taught them *"publicly and from house to house" (Acts 20:20).*

v. **Conference Circuit Christianity:** Some pastors spend more time speaking at conferences and events than shepherding their local congregation. While sharing wisdom with the broader church isn't wrong, many have become more like traveling celebrities than local church pastors. The early apostles maintained deep connections with local churches even while traveling to spread the gospel.

vi. **The Scandal Impact:** When celebrity pastors fall into sin or face scandal, the damage extends far beyond their local church. Recent years have seen numerous high-profile ministry collapses that have wounded thousands of believers and damaged the church's witness. Because these leaders built ministries around their personalities rather than Christ, their moral failures have far-reaching consequences.

vii. **Financial Extravagance:** We've witnessed pastors justifying private jets, multiple luxury homes, and expensive cars as "tools for ministry." *This lifestyle not only contradicts Jesus's example but also creates a stumbling block for both believers and unbelievers. Paul worked with his own hands to avoid being a burden to the church (1*

Thessalonians 2:9), yet some modern pastors live like celebrities while their congregants struggle financially.

viii. **The Leadership Pipeline Problem:** Many churches now hire only the students of celebrity pastors or those who match their "brand," creating a closed system that perpetuates personality-driven ministry rather than Spirit-led leadership. This contradicts the biblical pattern of recognizing spiritual gifts and calling within local congregations.

These issues reveal why we must return to biblical patterns of leadership. True pastoral ministry isn't about building platforms but about building people. It's not about creating brands but about creating disciples. As Jesus said, *"The good shepherd lays down his life for the sheep" (John 10:11)*.

The Dangerous Trend of Pastoral Inheritance

Another troubling aspect of modern church leadership is the assumption that ministry calling follows family bloodlines. We often see pastoral positions passed down from father to son, like a family business or royal inheritance. While God certainly can and does call multiple members of the same family to ministry, we must be careful not to assume that a pastor's children are automatically called to take over the pulpit.

Scripture shows us that spiritual leadership is based on God's calling, not family succession. Moses's sons didn't inherit his leadership role - God chose Joshua, who wasn't his relative. Samuel's sons weren't fit to lead (1 Samuel 8:1-3) despite their father's profound ministry. In the New Testament, we see Timothy serving not because he inherited a position but because Paul recognized God's genuine calling in his life.

The idea that pastoral ministry should automatically pass to the next generation creates several problems:

It can force individuals into roles they're not called to fulfill. Many pastors' children feel pressured to enter ministry despite lacking a genuine calling, leading to burnout, resentment, and sometimes even loss of faith.

It ignores the sovereign work of the Holy Spirit in calling leaders. *Acts 13:2* demonstrates that the Holy Spirit specifically calls individuals to ministry: ***"While they were worshiping the Lord and fasting, the Holy Spirit said, 'Set apart for me Barnabas and Saul for the work to which I have called them.'"***

It can perpetuate unhealthy leadership patterns. When churches automatically install pastors' children as successors, they may overlook serious character issues or lack of qualification simply because of family connections. Paul's leadership qualifications in 1 Timothy 3 and Titus 1 never mention family lineage as a factor.

We've seen the tragic results of this practice in many modern churches. Large ministries crumble because an unqualified son was given leadership solely based on being "the pastor's kid." Congregations suffer when genuine calling is superseded by family obligation. The gospel's advancement is hindered when ministry becomes about preserving family legacy rather than following God's leading.

Ministry calling must come from God, not genealogy. ***Jeremiah 23:21*** warns***, "I did not send these prophets, yet they have run with their message; I did not speak to them, yet they have prophesied."*** This applies to those who enter the ministry because of family pressure rather than a divine calling.

True pastoral succession should be based on the following:

- Clear evidence of God's calling
- Meeting biblical leadership qualifications
- Demonstration of spiritual maturity
- Confirmation from the body of Christ
- Genuine heart for ministry, not obligation

Being a pastor's child might provide unique insights into ministry, but it doesn't automatically equate to a calling. Each believer must discover and follow their calling, whether that leads to pulpit ministry or another form of service in God's kingdom.

8

The Power of True Worship: Beyond Entertainment

Worship is one of the most profound aspects of our relationship with God, yet It has become one of the most misunderstood aspects of modern church life. Many churches today have transformed their sanctuaries into concert venues, complete with elaborate light shows, fog machines, and concert-style productions. Yet Jesus declared in ***John 4:23-24, "But the hour is coming, and is now here, when the true worshipers will worship the Father in spirit and truth, for the Father is seeking such people to worship him. God is spirit, and those who worship him must worship in spirit and truth."***

This passage reminds us that worship is not about external effects but about connecting deeply with God in authenticity and truth. Yet, walk into numerous modern services, and you'll find:

- Sanctuaries intentionally darkened to create "atmosphere"
- Fog machines creating a concert environment
- Elaborate light shows that rival rock concerts

- Professional-level sound systems focused on entertainment
- Worship teams that perform rather than lead
- Congregations that watch rather than participate

These trends raise an important question: Are we worshiping God or creating an experience for ourselves? Scripture says, ***"God is light; in him there is no darkness at all" (1 John 1:5).*** Why create an artificial atmosphere when the Holy Spirit's presence is all we need?

True worship isn't about creating the right mood through external effects. The early church worshipped powerfully without any of these modern additions. ***Acts 2:46-47*** tells us they worshipped ***"with glad and sincere hearts, praising God and enjoying the favor of all the people."*** Their focus wasn't on the environment but on God Himself.

The danger in entertainment-style worship lies not only in its methods but in what it does to our understanding of worship itself:

1. It creates spectators rather than participants
2. It emphasizes emotional experience over spiritual truth
3. It can mask the absence of genuine Holy Spirit presence
4. It shifts focus from God to performance
5. It can become addictive, requiring ever-increasing stimulation

Consider how Jesus described the Temple: ***"My house shall be called a house of prayer" (Matthew 21:13)***—not a house of entertainment, not a concert venue, but a house of prayer. When we prioritize entertainment over encounter, we risk losing the very essence of worship.

Some argue these modern methods help reach young people or make the church more relevant. But we must ask: Are we creating genuine disciples or merely attracting crowds? Are we fostering true worship or feeding a desire for entertainment? Jesus never commanded us to make church entertaining; He commanded us to make disciples.

True worship, according to Scripture, should be:

- Spirit-led rather than performance-driven
- Truth-centered rather than emotion-dependent
- Participatory rather than observational
- God-focused rather than audience-focused
- Authentic rather than artificially created

Remember, the same Jesus who cleared the temple of money changers might have something to say about turning His house into a concert venue. This doesn't mean we can't use modern instruments or technology, but these should support worship, not become the focus of it.

The early church's worship was powerful not because of external elements but because of its authenticity. They ***"devoted themselves to the apostles' teaching and fellowship, to the breaking of bread and prayer" (Acts 2:42).*** Notice there's no mention of creating the right atmosphere or using special effects.

How can churches return to authentic worship? Let's examine practical steps toward restoring true worship in our churches.

First, we must understand that genuine worship can happen in a simple setting, and there's no need for other extravagant settings. Some of the most powerful moves of God have occurred in basic buildings with minimal equipment. When Paul and Silas worshipped in prison (Acts 16:25-26), they had no instruments, no light shows, no sound system - yet their authentic worship shook the prison's foundations.

Churches can begin by literally bringing light back into God's house. Turn the lights on during worship. Let people see each other's faces as they worship together as a family. Let children see their parents' worship. Allow the congregation to read their Bibles without using phone flashlights. As Scripture says, ***"For you were once darkness, but now you are light in the Lord. Walk as children of light" (Ephesians 5:8).***

Consider rearranging your worship space to encourage participation rather than spectatorship. When the worship team becomes less visible and the congregation more engaged, something powerful happens. The focus shifts from platform to presence, from performance to praise.

Train worship leaders to be facilitators of worship rather than performers. True worship leaders don't perform for the congregation; they help guide them into God's presence. This means selecting songs that congregations can sing, maintaining singable keys, and choosing lyrics that align with Scripture.

Implement times of spontaneous worship where the Holy Spirit can lead. This might mean leaving space in the worship service for prayer, testimony, or simply waiting on God. Not everything needs to be scripted and programmed. As Paul wrote, ***"Where the Spirit of the Lord is, there is freedom" (2 Corinthians 3:17).***

Create opportunities for congregational participation beyond singing. This could include Scripture reading, corporate prayer, or times of testimony. When people actively participate in worship rather than passively observe, they engage more deeply with God and each other.

Most importantly, teach your congregation about true worship. Help them understand that worship isn't just singing songs - it's an encounter with the living God. Explain that while emotions may be present in worship, they shouldn't be the focus or validation of worship.

Remember, the goal isn't to completely reject modern tools but to ensure they serve worship rather than dominate it. A simple sound system that helps people hear clearly is different from an elaborate production that overwhelms the senses. Technology should facilitate worship, not become the focus of it.

True revival has never depended on special effects or professional productions. It comes when God's people humble themselves, pray, seek His face, and turn from their wicked ways (2 Chronicles 7:14). As we return to these fundamental principles, we'll discover that authentic worship has a power that no number of special effects can replicate.

Finding Biblical Balance with Modern Technology

Let me be clear: this message isn't against using modern technology in worship. God can certainly be glorified through the proper use of contemporary tools and instruments. The issue isn't the tools themselves but how we use them. As Solomon built the temple with the finest materials and craftsmanship of his day, we too can use the best tools of our time to facilitate worship - but they must serve the purpose of worship, not overshadow it.

Modern sound systems serve an important purpose - helping people clearly hear the Word of God and participate in corporate worship. Professional lighting can be used effectively without turning the sanctuary into a concert venue. The key is balance. We can use stage lighting to help people see those leading worship while keeping the congregation well-lit for active participation. Rather than darkness and fog, we can use tasteful lighting that enhances the worship environment while maintaining the light and transparency that Scripture calls us to demonstrate.

Video screens can be valuable tools for displaying Scripture and song lyrics, making it easier for everyone to participate in worship. Live streaming technology allows us to reach shut-ins and share God's Word with those who can't physically attend. These are meaningful uses of technology that serve the body of Christ rather than entertain it.

Even contemporary worship music and modern instruments can be powerful tools when used properly. David used the most current instruments of his day to praise God. The problem isn't using current music styles or instruments - it's allowing the musical experience to overshadow the worship experience. When the drum fill becomes more important than the Holy Spirit's filling, we've lost our way.

Think of technology like a microphone - it should amplify worship, not alter its substance. Just as a microphone helps people hear better without changing the message, our modern tools should enhance worship without transforming it into entertainment. We can embrace technological advances while maintaining the purity and authenticity of true worship.

We must constantly ask, "Does this tool serve worship, or has worship begun to serve the tool?" When used correctly, modern technology can help eliminate distractions rather than create them, allowing people to focus more fully on God rather than less.

9

RETURNING TO BIBLICAL FOUNDATIONS

In an era where churches chase cultural relevance and adapt to modern trends, we must remember Jesus's words about building on solid ground in ***Matthew 7:24-25: "Therefore everyone who hears these words of mine and puts them into practice is like a wise man who built his house on the rock. The rain came down, the streams rose, and the winds blew and beat against that house, yet it did not fall because it had its foundation on the rock."***

These words remind us that the church's strength and endurance depend on its foundation. Yet today, many churches are shifting away from their biblical roots in pursuit of growth, popularity, or acceptance. We see this in multiple ways:

Bible teaching has been reduced to motivational speeches. Many pulpits now offer self-help messages sprinkled with Scripture rather than solid biblical exposition. Paul's instruction to Timothy remains crucial: ***"Preach the word; be prepared in season and out of season; correct, rebuke and encourage—with great patience and careful instruction" (2 Timothy 4:2).***

Prayer has become an afterthought rather than a foundation. The early church was birthed in a prayer meeting (Acts 1:14) and sustained by prayer (Acts 2:42). Yet many modern churches schedule only brief moments for prayer, treating it as a ceremonial opening rather than the vital foundation it should be.

Discipleship has been replaced with entertainment. Jesus commanded us to "make disciples" (Matthew 28:19), not to create audiences. True discipleship involves teaching believers to to obey all of Jesus's commands, even when they are challenging.

Fellowship has been reduced to casual socializing. The deep, sacrificial community described in Acts 2:44-45 bears little resemblance to the superficial connections found in many modern churches. Real biblical fellowship involves sharing life, resources, and spiritual growth.

Returning to biblical foundations means:

i. **Understanding God's Word:** Churches must go beyond reading Scripture to studying and faithfully applying it. We must follow the example of the Bereans, who **"examined the Scriptures every day to see if what Paul said was true" (Acts 17:11).**

ii. **Prioritizing Prayer:** Prayer should permeate every aspect of church life, just as it did in the early church. Before programs, strategies, and activities, prayer must come first.

iii. **Practicing True Fellowship:** Fellowship means more than socializing. It involves believers sharing their lives, bearing one another's burdens (Galatians 6:2) and encouraging one another toward love and good deeds (Hebrews 10:24-25).

iv. **Emphasizing Discipleship:** Moving beyond Sunday services to intentional, relational discipleship that transforms lives through the power of God's Word and Spirit.

Perhaps most importantly, returning to biblical foundations means restoring the centrality of Jesus Christ in all we do. Paul reminded the Colossians that Christ is ***"before all things, and in him all things hold together" (Colossians 1:17).*** Every program, service, and activity must be centered on and flow from our relationship with Christ.

Practical Steps for Returning to Biblical Foundations

First and foremost, churches must return to expository preaching of God's Word. This means working through Scripture systematically rather than cherry-picking verses to support popular topics. As Paul instructed in *2 Timothy 2:15*, we must be those who ***"correctly handle the word of truth."*** This involves:

Teaching through entire books of the Bible, allowing Scripture to set the agenda rather than current events or popular trends. When congregations understand the full context of Scripture, they're better equipped to discern truth from error.

Churches need to restore genuine prayer meetings—not just quick prayer before service but dedicated times where the congregation gathers specifically to pray. Consider how the early church responded to persecution *in Acts 4:23-31* — they gathered to pray, and *"the place where they were meeting was shaken."* Modern churches must create space for such powerful corporate prayer.

Biblical discipleship must be reestablished. Jesus spent three years pouring into His disciples, teaching them not just through words but through life examples.

Churches should develop intentional discipleship paths that include:

- One-on-one mentoring relationships
- Small group Bible studies focused on application, not just information
- Regular accountability among believers
- Practical training in spiritual disciplines

The restoration of true fellowship requires creating opportunities for deeper connection. *Acts 2:46* tells us the early church met *"every day"* in homes.

While daily meetings might not be practical today, churches can:

- Encourage regular small group meetings in homes
- Create opportunities for intergenerational fellowship

- Foster environments where genuine relationships can develop
- Provide space for believers to share testimonies and life experiences

Biblical church leadership must be restored according to scriptural qualifications. This means:

- Appointing leaders based on character rather than charisma
- Ensuring leaders meet the qualifications outlined in 1 Timothy 3 and Titus 1
- Establishing proper accountability structures
- Training leaders in biblical principles rather than business models

Churches must return to the practice of church discipline as outlined in Matthew 18:15-17. This doesn't mean becoming judgmental but rather loving enough to confront sin and restore fallen brothers and sisters.

True worship must be restored as a lifestyle, not just a Sunday activity. Romans 12:1 calls us to offer our bodies as living sacrifices - this is our true worship. Churches should teach and model:

- Daily devotion to God
- Worship through obedience
- Living sacrificially
- Serving others as an act of worship

The ordinances of baptism and communion must be restored to their proper significance rather than treated as mere traditions. These sacred acts should be explained, honored, and practiced with reverence and understanding.

Finally, churches must recover their missionary zeal. The early church was passionate about spreading the gospel, even amid persecution. Modern churches need to:

- Train members in evangelism
- Support missions both locally and globally
- Encourage every member to see themselves as a missionary in their sphere of influence
- Prioritize the Great Commission in budget and programming

Remember, returning to biblical foundations isn't about recreating first-century practices exactly but about applying biblical principles in our current context. As Jesus said in *Matthew 13:52*, we should be like *"the owner of a house who brings out of his storeroom new treasures as well as old."*

10

Standing Firm in Truth: A Call to Action

As we conclude this examination of truth and deception in today's church, we are at a critical moment that demands decisive action. It's no longer enough to simply attend church - we must become active participants in protecting and preserving biblical truth.

Your first responsibility as a believer is to thoroughly examine what your church is teaching. Don't just accept what you hear from the pulpit. Instead, emulate the Bereans, who ***"examined the Scriptures every day to see if what Paul said was true" (Acts 17:11).*** When your church presents a teaching, ask yourself:

- Can they support it with Scripture in the proper context?
- Does it align with the whole of God's Word?
- Is Jesus Christ central to the message?

If you find that questions about teachings are discouraged or dismissed, consider it a serious warning sign. Any church that resists biblical examination or questioning is showing signs of potential deception. Jesus never feared questions, and neither should today's church leaders.

Pay attention to how your church handles key issues such as money, manages power, and treats those who disagree. If leadership becomes defensive when questioned about finances, demands unquestioning loyalty, or shames those who raise concerns, these are serious warning signs that shouldn't be ignored.

Don't hesitate to leave a church that strays from biblical truth. Don't remain in spiritually unhealthy environments out of guilt, tradition, or fear of change. Remember, your spiritual health and that of your family are more important than maintaining membership in a church that's departed from sound doctrine.

Use the SPIRIT Test we discussed earlier to evaluate your church's teachings:

- **S** - Scripture Alignment Does everything align with God's Word?
- **P** - Prophetic Accuracy: Are prophecies biblical and Christ-centered?
- **I** - Integrity in Leadership: Is there transparency and accountability?
- **R** - Reliable Gospel Is the true gospel being preached?
- **I** - Income Focus: Is there excessive emphasis on money?
- **T** - True to Jesus. Is Jesus Christ central in all things?

A Personal Challenge

I challenge you today to:

1. Read your Bible daily, becoming grounded in God's Word
2. Question teachings that don't align with Scripture
3. Apply the SPIRIT Test to messages you hear
4. Have the courage to stand against false teaching
5. Find a church that teaches biblical truth without compromise
6. Help others who may be trapped in deceptive teachings

Remember, standing for truth isn't about being argumentative or judgmental. It's about protecting the purity of the gospel and helping others find freedom in God's truth. As Paul wrote to the Galatians, ***"It is for freedom that Christ has set us free. Stand firm, then, and do not let yourselves be burdened again by a yoke of slavery" (Galatians 5:1).***

The time for passive Christianity is over. We must engage, examine, and act. Whether through diligent study of Scripture, asking hard questions at your church, or guiding others toward biblical truth, you have a vital role to play in these critical times.

Don't stay silent when you encounter false teaching, don't ignore red flags in your church, and don't prioritize comfort over truth. The stakes are too high, and the consequences too eternal for such passivity.

Take action today. Study God's Word, test everything you hear, and stand firm in truth. The future of the church depends on believers who are willing to defend biblical truth, regardless of the cost.

NEW BELIEVER'S GUIDE: TAKING YOUR NEXT STEPS

If you are a new believer reading this book, you might feel overwhelmed by all the information presented. This guide will help you apply what you've learned in practical, manageable steps, ensuring your spiritual journey begins on a firm foundation.

Understanding Sound Doctrine (Chapters 1-3): The foundation of your faith journey begins with daily Bible reading. Don't feel pressured to understand everything immediately - this is a journey of growth. Start with the Gospel of John to learn about Jesus's life, teachings, and purpose. Then move to the Book of Acts to understand how the early church developed and operated. Keep the SPIRIT Test close as your companion when listening to any teaching or choosing a church.

Church Life (Chapters 4-6): Choosing the right church is crucial for your spiritual growth. Look for a church that teaches directly from the Bible and welcomes questions about its teachings. The church should demonstrate financial transparency and focus on Jesus rather than building up personalities. Most importantly, it should encourage you to read and study Scripture for yourself rather than depend solely on the pastor's interpretation.

Worship and Growth (Chapters 7-9): True worship extends far beyond Sunday services - it's a lifestyle of devotion to God. Begin your journey with simple, manageable steps. Start each day with prayer, even if it's just a few minutes. Practice thanking God throughout your day for His presence and blessings. Make reading at least one Bible chapter part of your daily routine. These habits will help build a strong foundation for your faith.

Two crucial steps for growth:

- Find a mature believer who can mentor you
- Join a Bible study group where you can ask questions and learn from others

Standing Firm (Chapter 10): Remember, growing in faith is a journey, not a race. Focus on building a strong foundation in God's Word through consistent study and prayer. Learn to recognize truth from error using the principles we've discussed. Most importantly, don't try to walk this path alone - develop relationships with other believers who can encourage and support your growth.

Resources for Growth: Your most important tool will be a study Bible in a translation you can understand. Consider starting a prayer journal to record your spiritual journey, questions, and God's faithfulness in your life. Don't hesitate to use the SPIRIT Test when evaluating teachings, and never be afraid to ask questions - seeking understanding is part of growth.

Remember, everyone starts somewhere in their faith journey. Jesus doesn't expect you to know everything at once. Focus on building your relationship with Him through prayer and Bible study, and trust the Holy Spirit to guide you into all truth, just as Jesus promised in Jo and God commands that repentance and essential for the forgiveness of sins. I believe that justification, regeneration, and the new birth are wrought by faith in the blood of Jesus Christ. Sanctification follows the new birth through faith in Christ's blood, God's Word, and these scriptures:

First, we must acknowledge our need for salvation: *"For all have sinned and fall short of the glory of God" (Romans 3:23).*

We must understand sin's consequence: *"For the wages of sin is death, but the gift of God is eternal life in Christ Jesus our Lord" (Romans 6:23).*

Yet God provided the solution: *"But God demonstrates his love for us in this: While we were still sinners, Christ died for us" (Romans 5:8).*

The path to salvation is clear: *"If you declare with your mouth, 'Jesus is Lord,' and believe in your heart that God raised him from the dead, you will be saved" (Romans 10:9).*

And the promise is for everyone: *"Everyone who calls on the name of the Lord will be saved" (Romans 10:13).*

Prayer of Salvation:

"Dear Heavenly Father,

I come to You knowing that I am a sinner. I believe that Your Son, Jesus Christ, died for my sins, that He was buried, and that You raised Him from the dead. I turn from my sins now and ask You to forgive me. I confess Jesus as my Lord and Savior. I will follow Him as Lord of my life from this day forward. Fill me with Your Holy Spirit, and help me to live for You.

In Jesus' name, Amen."

Name: _____

Date: _____

Keep this as a reminder of the day you began your journey with Christ. Remember, this is not just a one-time prayer but the beginning of a lifelong relationship with Jesus.

STATEMENT OF FAITH, UNDERSTANDING OF GRACE, AND CONTACT INFORMATION

I believe in the verbal inspiration of the Bible, God's holy and infallible Word. My faith rests in one God who eternally exists in three persons: the Father, Son, and Holy Ghost. I firmly believe that Jesus Christ is the only begotten Son of the Father, conceived of the Holy Ghost and born of the Virgin Mary. Jesus was crucified, buried, and gloriously resurrected from the dead. Today, He ascends to the right hand of the Father, where He serves as our Intercessor.

Scripture teaches us that all have sinned and fallen short of God's glory, and that repentance is commanded by God and essential for the forgiveness of sins. I believe that justification, regeneration, and the new birth are wrought by faith in the blood of Jesus Christ. Sanctification follows the new birth through faith in Christ's blood, through God's Word, and by the Holy Ghost. God's standard for His people is holiness in daily living.

God's grace manifests in three distinct and transformative ways:

i. Prevenient grace is God's divine initiative, present even before our awareness of Him. This grace draws us toward

God even before we consciously seek Him, preparing our hearts for the realization of His immense love for us. It's God's first step in pursuing a relationship with us.

ii. Justifying grace manifests when we cease trying to earn God's favor through our efforts. By placing our faith fully in Jesus Christ, we receive His forgiveness and pardon. This grace brings peace, joy, and love as we experience God's complete acceptance and forgiveness.

iii. Sanctifying grace is God's ongoing work in our lives. It transforms us into Christ's image and leads us toward both inward and outward holiness. This grace enables our continued spiritual growth and maturation in faith.

I believe in the baptism with the Holy Ghost subsequent to a clean heart and that speaking in other tongues as the Spirit gives utterance is the initial evidence of this baptism. Water baptism should be by immersion, and all who repent should be baptized in the name of the Father, Son, and Holy Ghost.

My faith embraces divine healing as provided for all in the atonement, and I uphold the observance of the Lord's Supper and washing of the saint's feet. I anticipate the premillennial second coming of Jesus—first, to resurrect the righteous dead and catch away the living saints to Him in the air, and second, to reign on earth for a thousand years. I believe in bodily resurrection, with eternal life for the righteous and eternal punishment for the wicked.

Contact Information: For questions, discussions, or to contact this ministry, please email me at *cj-lester@outlook.com*. I welcome thoughtful dialogue and the opportunity to share God's truth with others seeking authentic biblical teaching.

Made in the USA
Columbia, SC
22 February 2025

0b318211-1919-4d49-bc87-26df902bbbfeR01